PSALMS
VOLUME 2

Living Word BIBLE STUDIES

Joshua: All God's Good Promises

Nehemiah: Rebuilt and Rebuilding

Psalms, Volume 1: Songs along the Way

Psalms, Volume 2: Finding the Way to Prayer and Praise

Proverbs: The Ways of Wisdom

Ecclesiastes and Song of Songs: Wisdom's Searching and Finding

Isaiah: The Lord Saves

John: That You May Believe

Colossians and Philemon: Continue to Live in Him

1 & 2 Thessalonians: Living the Gospel to the End

PSALMS

VOLUME 2

*Finding the Way
to Prayer and Praise*

KATHLEEN BUSWELL NIELSON

P&R
PUBLISHING
P.O. BOX 817 • PHILLIPSBURG • NEW JERSEY 08865-0817

ISBN: 978-1-59638-587-2

Printed in the United States of America

CONTENTS

Foreword by David R. Helm   vii
A Personal Word from Kathleen   ix
Introduction   xi

LESSON 1 (PSALM 2)
Remembering the Way of the Psalms   1

LESSON 2 (PSALMS 11 & 12)
The Way through a Wicked World   17

LESSON 3 (PSALMS 19 & 8)
The Way of Glorious Revelation   31

LESSON 4 (PSALMS 56 & 57)
The Way of Praise for Deliverance   45

LESSON 5 (PSALMS 51 & 130)
The Way of Repentance   57

LESSON 6 (PSALMS 66 & 67)
The Way of Large Praise   69

LESSON 7 (PSALMS 85 & 126)
The Way between Already and Not Yet   81

CONTENTS

LESSON 8 (PSALMS 86 & 138)
The Way of Trusting in Trouble   93

LESSON 9 (PSALMS 92 & 93)
The Way of Praise to God on High   105

LESSON 10 (PSALMS 81 & 95)
The Way of Exhortation   117

LESSON 11 (PSALMS 102 & 94)
The Way of Farsighted Lament   129

LESSON 12 (PSALMS 147 & 148)
The Way through God's World   141

Notes for Leaders   155
Notes on Translation and Study Helps   160

FOREWORD

David, Michelangelo's masterwork, was unveiled in Florence in the year 1504. The marble statue stands seventeen feet tall and is a most powerful sculpture. Strong in every respect, *David* is chiseled with an intensity that captures the biblical hero's confidence. The eyes are fixed, his head is turned toward the left, and the famous sling is held in his left hand, falling over his left shoulder. The general impression is of a young man fully capable of slaying a giant.

The real David lived some 2500 years before Michelangelo chiseled his image. His strength was not limited to the making of war; he was also a master of words. The book of 2 Samuel remembers him as "the sweet psalmist of Israel" (23:1), an apt title indeed! The real David was not merely God's anointed warrior king, but a musician, a shepherd boy, and a poet—a man of letters before the world had many of them.

Michelangelo and the real David both created masterful art, one using marble and one using words. One cut a figure from stone and one shaped verses to stir the soul. Like Michelangelo's art, David's art, that of writing masterful poetry, is a difficult skill to practice well. That said, it doesn't follow that we shouldn't learn how to *read* poetry well. In fact, with a willing spirit and a well-informed teacher, you and I can learn to read the poetry of the Bible in ways that nourish our lives.

This is precisely where Kathleen Nielson's training comes in. In this second volume on selected psalms, Nielson mentors us in the ways of poetry, David's favorite form of expression. In doing so, she equips us to get the most out of this biblical genre—whether or not David was the author of the particular psalm we are reading! With her expertise in literature and the English language, Kathleen understands how poetry works and why it is often the best medium for teaching us the wonders of God's ways. She leads us into the Psalms, a book of poetry that sends the lifeblood of God's Spirit back into our marbled souls.

David R. Helm
Pastor, Holy Trinity Church, Hyde Park
Chairman, The Charles Simeon Trust

A Personal Word
from Kathleen

I began to write these Bible studies for the women in my own church group at College Church in Wheaton, Illinois. Under the leadership of Kent and Barbara Hughes, the church and that Bible study aimed to proclaim without fail the good news of the Word of God. What a joy, in that study and in many since, to see lives changed by the work of the Word, by the Spirit, for the glory of Christ.

In our Bible study group, we were looking for curriculum that would lead us into the meat of the Word and teach us how to take it in, whole Bible books at a time—the way they are given to us in Scripture. Finally, one of our leaders said, "Kathleen—how about if you just write it!" And so began one of the most joyful projects of my life: the writing of studies intended to help unleash the Word of God in people's lives. The writing began during a busy stage of my life—with three lively young boys and always a couple of college English courses to teach—but through that stage and every busy one since, a serious attention to studying the Bible has helped keep me focused, growing, and alive in the deepest ways. The Word of God will do that. If there's life and power in these studies, it is simply the life and power of the Scriptures to which they point. It is ultimately the life and power of the Savior who shines through all the Scriptures from beginning to end. How we need this life, in the midst of every busy and non-busy stage of our lives!

I don't think it is just the English teacher in me that leads me to this conclusion about our basic problem in Bible study these days: we've forgotten how to *read!* We're so used to fast food that we think we should be able to drive by the Scriptures periodically and pick up some easily digestible truths that someone else has wrapped up neatly for us. We've disowned that process of careful reading . . . observing the words . . . seeing the shape of a book and a passage . . . asking questions that take us into the text rather than away from it . . . digging into the Word and letting it speak! Through such a process, guided by the Spirit, the Word of God truly feeds our souls. Here's my prayer: that, by means of these studies, people would be further enabled to read the Scriptures profitably and thereby find life and nourishment in them, as we are each meant to do.

In all the busy stages of life and writing, I have been continually surrounded by pastors, teachers, and family who encourage and help me in this work, and for that I am grateful. The most wonderful guidance and encouragement come from my husband, Niel, whom I thank and for whom I thank God daily.

May God use these studies to lift up Christ and his Word, for his glory!

INTRODUCTION

Hearing requests for a second volume on the Psalms, I have responded that the first volume was meant to encourage readers to study all the rest of the psalms on their own! However, through becoming more involved not just in teaching Bible studies but also in teaching others how to study the Bible, I have realized that it would be helpful to offer more explicit direction in learning how to study the Psalms. That's what this second volume aims to do, in a quite basic way.

The goal here is to take in deeply another representative selection of psalms, and to learn more about how to take them in. This volume exposes some of the process beneath the surface of the other studies—which on the one hand gives more help to readers, and on the other hand enables them to work more on their own.[1] After the introductory Lesson One, each lesson guides the study of one psalm and then provides the tools in Day Four for more independent study of another thematically related psalm. Each lesson ends with looking back over the two psalms studied and hiding some of their words in our hearts.

The Psalms teach God's people how to praise and pray. These 150 poems are the well-worn hymnbook and prayer book of

---

1. Considerations such as these led me to write *Bible Study: Following the Ways of the Word* (Phillipsburg, NJ: P&R Publishing, 2011), which might be helpful for those who wish to think further about why and how we study the Bible. I would also recommend *Dig Deeper*, by Nigel Beynon and Andrew Sach (Wheaton: Crossway, 2010).

generations of those who have put their faith in the one Lord God. The Psalms were gathered in various collections as early as the time of Moses and written mainly during the days of the kingdom, but the final form was probably established by those who served in the rebuilt temple after the exiled Jews had returned to Jerusalem. Lesson One of this study establishes the central context of the kingdom and the most common author, King David. Suffice it to say here that this Spirit-inspired poetry is *from* God's gathered people and *for* God's gathered people— from back in Old Testament times all the way to now, in the church today. What better proof than these enduring psalms that the one true God has been working throughout human history to redeem a people for himself, through his anointed King.

These psalms will indeed point us to God's redemptive plan accomplished by his anointed King Jesus. We must begin studying, though, not by looking far ahead but by looking carefully into the text of each psalm. The aim will be to take in the words of the psalms as carefully as possible—relishing the poetic language, the shape of each psalm, its meaning in its original form and context. The beautiful truth is that we don't have to impose the light of Jesus on the psalms. When we study them deeply, we find they connect us deeply, on many levels, to the Lord God who made us and loves us and saves us through his Son. God's redemptive plan shines out from the heart of the psalms. The more we understand them, the more they turn our thoughts (sometimes directly and sometimes more indirectly) to the promised Christ who came; who died for us, bearing our sin; who rose again, conquering death; and who reigns in heaven until that day when he comes again to judge the earth and to reign forever with his people. As we study, the psalms begin to resonate with the story of redemption that holds Scripture together from beginning to end. They are at the heart of that story, as they express the heartfelt prayers and praises of a people in need of a Redeemer God.

Starting with the text also means we will not start by offering our personal responses to the text. We'll aim first to look neither far ahead nor deep inside ourselves, but rather into the words God inspired. If we start there, we can hope to end up, by God's grace, with the most profound and appropriate sorts of personal responses—ones that grow out of hearing God's voice in his Word.

How crucial to remember that our study of the Bible is never just academic or purely intellectual. To study God's Word is to lean in close to the very breath of God as, by his Spirit, these living and active words reveal him to us. I know of no better balm for the heart than to listen well to God's voice that so mercifully speaks to us in his Word.

May we hear God speaking to us in the Psalms. May we learn better how to offer words of praise and prayer to him. And may we, at the conclusion of this study, be encouraged to study all the rest of the psalms on our own!

Lesson 1 (Psalm 2)

REMEMBERING THE
WAY OF THE PSALMS

This lesson aims to immerse us in the book of Psalms so that we will be ready to dig into individual psalms in the lessons ahead. Volume 1 used Psalm 1 in the introductory lesson; here in Volume 2 we will use Psalm 2, as we make our way into the riches of this book. To delight in and meditate on the Psalms is a lifelong process. It is good to step back from time to time in that process and remember just what makes up the book of Psalms. Here's one way to say it: *The Psalms are cries from the kingdom that focus on God the King, voicing the true experience of kingdom life through poetry fit for a King!*

DAY ONE—THE PSALMS ARE CRIES
FROM THE KINGDOM

1. The huge majority of psalms were composed in the context of the kingdom of Israel, with King David as the

most common writer. From the two following passages, what can you observe about this context of King David and the kingdom?

a.   2 Samuel 23:1–7

b.   1 Chronicles 16

2. As David led his people in worship of God, the Psalms formed a great part of that worship, often by being sung. The word *psalm* comes from the Greek translation of the Hebrew word for *song*.

   a.   Now that you've read 1 Chronicles 16, notice and comment on some of the psalms' titles, such as in Psalm 4: "To the choirmaster, with stringed instruments. A Psalm of David." Look specifically at Psalms 4–6 and 73–83.

b. How might all this historical context affect our reading and understanding of the Psalms?

3. David clearly knew he was inspired by God's Spirit to write these words (2 Sam. 23:2). As we approach the Psalms as part of the Scriptures breathed out by God, what are some of the implications for how we should study them (and perhaps also how we *shouldn't*)? (See also 2 Timothy 3:16.)

4. Like Saul before him, David was anointed as king. For background on the anointing of a king of Israel, read 1 Samuel 9:27–10:1 and 16:11–13. Then read Psalm 2:1–6. In relation to Israel's anointed kings, what is the main message here?

5. Day Two will unfold the kingdom further. For now, from both Psalm 1 and Psalm 2:1–6, list some of the very basic truths that emerge about God and about human beings. Psalms 1 and 2 have often been called the gateway into the book of Psalms: the truths established here at the start shape our perspective on all the psalms to come.

Day Two—The Psalms Focus on God the King

1. Numerous psalms celebrate the anointed king. Observe, for example, Psalm 45:1–7. Write several basic observations.

2. What happened to David's kingdom eventually? Skim the end of the story in 2 Chronicles 36.

3. But what had God promised David in 2 Samuel 7:12–17? This promise certainly refers to David's son, the great King Solomon, but how can we tell that it also refers to one greater than Solomon?

4. Now read Psalm 2:7–9, in which the anointed King actually speaks, echoing the promise to David that we just read. Then turn to the New Testament and read Hebrews 1:1–9 (not to understand every detail, but to get the main argument). What is Hebrews telling us about these Old Testament words?

5. The context of the whole Bible lets us understand that God has fully revealed himself in the promised King Jesus.

   a. Read God's words to Jesus in Mark 1:9–11. Read Jesus' words in Mark 1:14–15, as he begins his public earthly ministry. How do these verses help confirm that Psalm 2 is pointing to Jesus?

   b. What strong truths about this King emerge in Psalm 2:7–9?

The Psalms light up God the King: his creation of the world, his sovereign hand over all creation, his judgment of sin, and his promised forgiveness and deliverance for those who repent and turn to him. All these ways of God are made known to us fully in Jesus Christ his Son. The Psalms focus us on God—and they point us to Christ (sometimes quite directly, as in Psalm 2, and sometimes more indirectly). Finally, on this day, read and meditate on all of Psalm 2, in light of the fact that it points to Christ. (*Christ* comes from the Greek translation of the Hebrew *anointed*.)

Day Three—The Psalms Voice the True Experience of Kingdom Life

1. The Psalms light up the eternal King, but they do it in the voices and from the experience of real people living in his kingdom. Many have observed the amazing breadth of human experience touched on by the Psalms. Page through the first ten psalms, for example, skimming just the first few verses of each. What various experiences and tones do you find represented?

2. The Psalms are divided into five books, but they follow no clear logical order. Certain categories emerge (and sometimes overlap), such as royal psalms, messianic psalms, praise psalms, penitential psalms, wisdom psalms, psalms of lament, worship psalms, imprecatory psalms, and so forth. What truths about God and about ourselves might the breadth of these categories teach us?

3. God's people for centuries used the Psalms as regular texts for their prayers and praises in temple worship. Jesus would have used them in this way. Considering the Psalms' broad reach into human experience, in what ways might regular reading of them teach us how to pray and praise?

4. Psalm 119 is a prayer celebrating God's Word and asking God to help us walk in its light through all the experiences of life to the end. Read Psalm 119:25–40, praying these verses particularly in relation to your study of the Psalms. Write down and meditate on a couple of verses that stand out.

5. What kinds of prayers might Psalm 2 teach you to pray?

DAY FOUR—THE PSALMS GIVE US POETRY FIT FOR A KING!

The Psalms are poetry! This poetry is not just an extra decoration to be noticed if we have time. Studying the form of a psalm is a crucial part of studying (and delighting in) the meaning. We'll notice three aspects of this Old Testament poetry.

1. First, *poetic shape*. Poetry comes in various forms, but in the Psalms it comes in the form of 150 separate poems, each with its own shape from beginning to end. Sometimes the shape is quite clear; sometimes it's debatable. Sometimes there is more than one possible shape. If your Bible edition divides the text into sections for you, it's a good idea not always to take those divisions as fact but rather to read the text and see for yourself. Psalm 2 falls rather neatly into four sections—like a kind of drama in four acts, each with a distinct voice emerging.

   a. Identify four sections of Psalm 2. What title and brief description might you give to each one?

b. Now look at the four sections together, as they move from beginning to end of this poem. How do they hold together? Explain briefly how we might see these sections developing one main idea or train of thought.

As we look at each poem, we will aim to find its main idea—a central theme that holds it together from beginning to end. For Psalm 2, for example, we might conclude that the main idea is something like: *God has set his anointed King over all the nations.* That could sum up the four sections, which show three different perspectives on that anointed King followed by a warning about him. Another possibility might be: *God's anointed King over all nations will bring judgment on all who rebel.* The more we come to know the psalm and its whole shape, the more clearly we will be able to get at the main idea.

2. A second aspect of Hebrew poetry is *parallelism*. Hebrew poetry comes in parallel units of meaning, often two but sometimes three or more units, which in English

we see as lines on the page. Three kinds of parallelism are generally acknowledged:

- antithetic parallelism (The lines offer contrasting ideas.)
- synonymous parallelism (The lines offer similar ideas.)
- synthetic parallelism (The lines develop an idea from one line into the next, in a number of possible ways.)

Psalm 2 is full of synonymous parallelism, in which a second line basically repeats an idea, *but always with differences that deepen the meaning.* Find and comment on two examples of synonymous parallelism in Psalm 2.

3. A third aspect of this poetry is its *imagery.* Poetry in general uses concrete pictures to communicate—pictures like those of "bonds" and "cords" in Psalm 2:3.

    a. What do these pictures in Psalm 2:3 make you see and understand?

b. Sometimes pictures resonate throughout Scripture. (Think of bread, and water, and light, for example.) How might Hosea 11:4 help you process the pictures in Psalm 2:3?

c. What do the pictures in Psalm 2:9 make you see and understand?

4. About a third of the Bible is poetry—magnificent poetry, fit for a King! We enrich our understanding of God's Word when we notice the way the poetry communicates. Why do you think God filled his inspired Word with so much poetry?

DAY FIVE—TAKE IT IN

We've developed this summary of what makes up the book of Psalms: *The Psalms are cries from the kingdom that focus on God the King, voicing the true experience of kingdom life through poetry fit for a King!* We've glimpsed the promised King Jesus, who brought the kingdom to us; God sent his own Son (this King!) to dwell among us. It was this King who died in our place, the perfect sacrifice to accomplish the forgiveness of our sins.

One more thing needs to be clear: we are called to respond. Jesus came proclaiming the gospel and calling people to respond in faith. The whole Bible is God's voice to us, and by his Spirit we are called to respond.

1. The Psalms teach us well how to respond! For example, in the fourth and final section of Psalm 2, the psalmist calls kings and rulers to respond rightly to God's anointed King (see verse 10—and recall verse 2!). How might the kinds of responses in Psalm 2:10–12 be especially important for any kind of earthly ruler? How do these verses reach out to apply to any of us as well? Spend some moments in prayer, taking time to respond personally to your heavenly King.

2. The final day of each lesson will ask you to reread the psalm(s) studied and to choose a verse or passage you would like to memorize. Let's begin with Psalm 2. Write out your chosen verse or passage and commit it to memory (or begin to do so!). Make these words a part of your thinking and your prayers. Be ready, if you wish, to tell your group why you picked these words and how they are working in your heart. By the end of the study, with regular review, you should have a collection of personal treasures from the Psalms.

Thoughts and Observations—Psalm 11

Lesson 2 (Psalms 11 & 12)

THE WAY THROUGH
A WICKED WORLD

We begin to dig in! Before us are two psalms that vividly express the struggle to live as people who belong to God in a fallen world. Both are written by David and addressed "to the choirmaster," which reminds us of the general context of the worshiping kingdom of Israel (see Lesson One). David, who knew what it was like to meet threats on every side, here gives no specific historical context; rather, he articulates his experience, as God inspired him, in a way that could be used in worship by all God's people—even today. These psalms meet us in the real world where we live. Both of these psalms encourage us to be honest about our struggle *and* clear about our hope.

DAY ONE—READ AND OBSERVE

Each first day of these lessons will ask you not just to read through a psalm, but to read and reread and reread again—and observe with care.

17

- To begin, pray for understanding, perhaps using that prayer from Psalm 119:25–40 that we read last week.

- Then read through Psalm 11 without pause, taking it in as a whole. Reading silently is fine; reading out loud is great, too!

- Reread it several times, stopping to think and observe and marking words and sections that stand out to you. (If you don't like marking in your Bible, you might want to print out a copy of the psalm to mark up.)

- Finally, write down (on page 16) at least five initial observations concerning the words you read in this psalm. They can be the most basic sorts of observations. What do you notice? What stands out to you in this psalm?

Day Two—Getting the Idea

1. Now that you've read Psalm 11 several times, you're beginning to discover its *shape*. As we saw in Lesson One, Day Four, each psalm is a complete poem that moves in a certain configuration from beginning to end. Questions like the following can help uncover a psalm's shape (*and the notes in italics will help!*):

   a. Identify the two main sections of this poem, and give each one a title and brief description. *Note: The quoted words beginning in the last line of verse 1 extend through verse 3, in most texts.*

b. What patterns or repetitions of words do you find? Write your observations. *Note: This crucial question could also be used to determine the <u>characters</u> this poem is about! There are two main groups—and the "*Lord.*"*

c. Notice the beginning and ending of this poem. *Note: How do the first and last lines make "bookends" that are different and yet alike in their focus of hope?*

2. Obviously there's a crisis referred to in Psalm 11:1–3.

    a.   In general, what can you discern from the text about the nature of this crisis?

    b.   In the midst of this crisis, David is responding to a voice (the unidentified "you" of verse 1) that recommends a course of action he obviously questions. What questionable actions and attitudes does David hear this voice recommending to him in Psalm 11:1–3?

3. Consider how the two main parts of the poem work together. In what various and beautiful ways does Psalm 11:4–7 shoot down the negative voice quoted in verses 1–3?

4. Now that you have considered the sections and their logical flow, look back on the whole poem. What is this psalm mainly about? How might you state the main idea—the idea that holds together the different sections of Psalm 11?

DAY THREE—FILLING IN THE PICTURE

1. In Psalm 11, imagery (picture language) makes both the challenge and the response more vivid.

   a. Comment on the scene pictured in Psalm 11:2. What does it look like and feel like?

b. We can't see in the dark. But how does the picture of *seeing* grow throughout this poem, even through the final line?

c. What is the effect of the pictures in Psalm 11:6? (See related pictures in Genesis 19:24–25 and Isaiah 51:17.)

2. So . . . what *can* the righteous *do* (Ps. 11:3)? The whole of Psalm 11 helps us deal with this question.

a. Who is the only one directly declared to be righteous in this psalm? What details of Psalm 11:4 highlight just who this is? *Note: The name "Lord" is the Hebrew Yahweh—the covenant name for the God who rules and acts in redemptive history.*

b. How is Psalm 11:6 important in answering the question of what the righteous can do?

c. So who are "the righteous" referred to in Psalm 11, and what can they do? How does David show us, in the psalm's first and last lines, just what the righteous do?

3. In relation to "the righteous," we cannot help but look ahead to the full revelation of Scripture.

a. How does Romans 3:21–26 clarify who it is who has righteousness in himself and how sinful human beings come to share in his righteousness?

b. In light of Christ, how can we find even fuller meaning in this psalm's words about righteousness?

4. We've surely been taking these words personally all along, but, now that we've "dug into" the meaning a bit, let's think explicitly about application. Let's put ourselves into the picture. What does it mean to you that, when some form of wickedness threatens, God's people take refuge in their righteous, ruling God?

a. What sorts of wickedness-related threats do you or those around you face today?

b. What would this psalm tell us not to do? In what ways might you be tempted to follow the voice David hears in Psalm 11:1–3?

c. In what ways can we take to heart David's example in this psalm? How are you learning about this true refuge in a righteous, sovereign, and very personal Lord God?

DAY FOUR—DIG IN YOURSELF (PSALM 12)

Each Day Four will offer you the opportunity to apply these questions yourself to a different but similarly themed psalm. The goal will be simply to make your way as far as possible through the following questions. Don't be pressured by this day's work; read and observe the psalm, and then just get as far as you can. If you're working with a group, it will be enlightening and fun to share (as you have time) what you have found so far. Be encouraged that this process of "digging in" becomes increasingly rewarding with practice. And every psalm opens up more and more each time we come back to it. But we have to begin! The more we take time even to begin to peer into these living and active words, the more they open up to us and truly feed our souls.

For Psalm 12, then, consider the following questions and notes. Portions of the notes will always apply specifically to the psalm under consideration. All the questions are listed here at the start; you may take them in this order, but of course they often overlap and work together!

1. Upon prayerful reading and rereading, what initial <u>observations</u> would you make?

2. Who wrote this psalm, and how much do we know about the <u>context</u>?

3. What <u>shape</u> does this psalm have? *Note the beginning and ending, the progression of sections, and patterns and repetitions of words and ideas.*

4. Does a <u>main idea</u> begin to emerge? *Note: Keep coming back to this question as you make your way through the others.*

5. How do the <u>parallel lines</u> and the <u>imagery</u> communicate in this poem? *Note: In each psalm different elements will stand out. Note in Psalm 12:1–2, for example, the way both verses use a kind of synonymous parallelism to restate but deepen an idea. Notice of course the one main picture that shines out in this poem!*

6. In what ways does this psalm point us to <u>Christ</u>? *Note: The connection is not direct in this psalm. One might think, for example,*

of John 1:1 or John 8:31—or Revelation 19:11–16, which shows the Word of God, in shining purity, finally conquering the wicked.

7. What sorts of personal <u>applications and prayers</u> might you take away from this psalm?

(Continued from previous page)

Day Five—Take It In

Reread the two psalms you have studied in this lesson, and from them choose a verse or passage you would like to memorize. Write out the verse or passage and commit it to memory (or begin to do so!). Make these words a part of your thinking and your prayers. Be ready, if you wish, to share with your group why you chose these words and how they are working in your heart.

Thoughts and Observations—Psalm 19

- the heavens declare the glory of God. nothing is hidden from him and his creation declares his existence.

- making wise the simple

- God's way is more desirable/enjoyable than fine gold.

- Joy in his commands and reward to those who keep it

- Innocent from hidden faults (12)

Lesson 3 (Psalms 19 & 8)

THE WAY OF
GLORIOUS REVELATION

The Psalms are full of wonder at this majestic God who has shown himself to us. Glory is the showing forth of God's very being. Both psalms for this week celebrate God's glory revealed in nature. But they don't stop there, as we shall see. These two psalms of David help us see God's world with more godly eyes.

DAY ONE—READ AND OBSERVE

- To begin, pray for understanding, perhaps using that prayer from Psalm 119:25–40. (In the process of this study, you might explore the many similarly helpful prayers in Psalm 119.)
- Read through Psalm 19 without pause, taking it in as a whole.

- Reread it several times, stopping to think and observe and marking words and sections that stand out to you.

- Finally, write down (on page 30) at least five initial observations concerning the words you read in this psalm. They can be the most basic sorts of observations. What do you notice? What stands out to you in this psalm?

DAY TWO—GETTING THE IDEA

1. Psalm 19 has a beautiful shape! Divide this psalm into three sections, suggesting your own title and brief description of each.

- The glory of God visibly on earth
- God's Law the beauty of
- blameless

2. What logical progression do you see from the beginning to the end of Psalm 19, section by section? *Consider: How does the focus change and develop? Note, for example, changes in the way God is named and addressed.*

3. Draw your own simple picture of the shape or outline of Psalm 19.

4. Trace and comment on the pattern of words related to *speaking* and *words* throughout Psalm 19.

5. What is this psalm mainly about? How would you state the main idea—the idea that holds together the different sections of Psalm 19?

DAY THREE—FILLING IN THE PICTURE

1. Obviously nature does not use actual words. Consider what kind of speech David is talking about, poetically, in Psalm 19:1–6.

   a. What does nature communicate, according to Psalm 19:1–2? What specific words in the text help answer this question? (See also Romans 1:18–20.)

   b. What sets of parallel lines in Psalm 19:1–4 emphasize the comprehensiveness of nature's declaration— always, everywhere?

c. One part of nature, the sun, emerges as the supreme example. How is the sun pictured in Psalm 19:4–6? What do you see? What aspects of God's glory does the sun show?

2. Psalm 19:7 turns from general revelation to written revelation.

a. How might that picture of the sun serve as a kind of transition? In what ways is the law like the sun?

b. In Psalm 19:7–9, many teachers would ask you to find
    three sets of words: words for the "law" (the books of
    Moses, or God's Word as people in David's time would
    have had it), words describing the law, and action words
    stating what the law accomplishes. It's a good exercise,
    and one that can be done because of the beautiful par-
    allelism and symmetry of the lines. So . . . make three
    lists, then observe and comment on them!

c. Psalm 19:10–11 describes the value of God's Word as
    it is received by one of his own. First, meditate on the
    pictures bursting and oozing out of verse 10. How

do these lines communicate the overflowing worth and beauty of God's Word? How do you respond?

3. The psalm's final verses help us with our personal response.

    a. How might Psalm 19:11 serve as a kind of transition into the final verses of the poem?

    b. In the light and heat of God's revelation, what various truths about his own sin does the psalmist understand, according to Psalm 19:12–13?

     c.   But how can a sinner be declared blameless and innocent? Consider the final prayer in Psalm 19:14. What truth about God here is our only hope? (Read Ephesians 1:3–10 to find the full explanation of that glorious final word of Psalm 19:14.)

4. Consider the levels of response to this psalm. What if we responded by acknowledging just the first section (Ps. 19:1–6)? Or, what if we responded by acknowledging only the first two sections (vv. 1–11)? How might we observe such responses in our world today? In what ways can you respond completely to this whole beautiful psalm?

DAY FOUR—DIG IN YOURSELF (PSALM 8)

Review the introduction to Day Four in Lesson Two. This lesson asks you to look into a second psalm that involves God's revelation of himself in nature. It's similar to Psalm 19 in some ways but different in its emphasis. For Psalm 8, then, consider the following questions and notes.

1. Upon prayerful reading and rereading, what initial <u>observations</u> would you make?

2. Who wrote this psalm, and how much do we know about the <u>context</u>?

3. What <u>shape</u> does this psalm have? *Note the beginning and ending, the progression of sections, and patterns and repetitions of words and ideas.*

4. Does a <u>main idea</u> begin to emerge? *Note: Keep coming back to this question as you make your way through the others.*

5. How do the <u>parallel lines</u> and the <u>imagery</u> communicate in this poem? *Note: In each psalm, different elements will stand out. Psalm 8 works less with imagery and more with the shape of the argument laid out so evocatively by the lines. The framework of God's majestic name here enfolds all creation from heights to depths, with man crowned with honor at the very pinnacle.*

6. In what ways does this psalm point us to <u>Christ</u>? (See Hebrews 2:5–9.)

7. What sorts of personal <u>applications and prayers</u> might you take away from this psalm?

(Continued from previous page)

(Continued from previous page)

Day Five—Take It In

Reread the two psalms you have studied in this lesson, and from them choose a verse or passage you would like to memorize. Write out the verse or passage and commit it to memory (or begin to do so!). Make these words a part of your thinking and your prayers. Be ready, if you wish, to share with your group why you chose these words and how they are working in your heart.

Thoughts and Observations—Psalm 56

* when I am afraid...
  ↳ people of God were afraid.
    ↳ I <u>put</u> my trust in you.
       Action.
  * Because I trust in God I should not be afraid
      ↳ after remembering who God is.

- Remembering = this I know, that God is for me.

- when I am afraid
- I should not be afraid ? me
- what can man do to me? they

* He delivered my Soul from death.

Lesson 4 (Psalms 56 & 57)

THE WAY OF PRAISE
FOR DELIVERANCE

Over and over the Psalms show us a God who delivers us from evil. These cries from the kingdom are cries from people who belong to the King but are still walking on the (often hard) path of life, with enemies all around. These psalms acknowledge the enemies and praise the God who delivers us from them.

DAY ONE—READ AND OBSERVE

- To begin, pray—thanking God for these inspired words and asking to understand them. You might use Scripture from Psalm 119 or from other psalms you've been reading.
- Read through Psalm 56 without pause, taking it in as a whole.

- Reread it several times, stopping to think and observe, and marking words and sections that stand out to you.

- Finally, write down (on page 44) at least five initial observations concerning the words you read in this psalm. They can be the most basic sorts of observations. What do you notice? What stands out to you in this psalm?

Day Two—Getting the Idea

1. First, let's consider this psalm's specific context. After some directions relating to the context of musical worship, the heading points us to 1 Samuel 21:10–22:2. What light does this passage shed on Psalm 56?

2. Divide Psalm 56 into four sections, suggesting your own title and brief description of each.

3. The first section introduces the three main characters (one is a group of characters) involved in this psalm.

   a. Who are these three main characters, and how does each subsequent section focus mainly on one of them?

   b. Now that you've seen the progression of the sections, summarize the logical argument at work from the beginning to the end of this poem. (Notice the posture or situation of the speaker at the beginning and then at the end.)

4. Trace and comment on the patterns and repetitions of words and phrases you find in this psalm. (Notice even in the first section the pairs of words that work together—and the refrain that gets echoed later almost word for word.)

5. What is this psalm mainly about? How would you state the main idea of Psalm 56?

DAY THREE—FILLING IN THE PICTURE

1. Psalm 56:1–4 introduces the poem with a kind of microcosm (a miniature form) of the whole psalm's movement.

   a. What details in Psalm 56:1–2 make the problem really vivid?

b. How does the psalmist communicate the process of his response in the progressive lines of Psalm 56:3–4?

c. Note and comment briefly on words that stand out in this introductory section.

2. In an almost ironic answer to the final question of verse 4, what consumes the speaker's attention in Psalm 56:5–7? How would you describe the tone and the perspective of these verses?

3. Psalm 56:8–11 brings a change in focus, perhaps introduced by the last line (or last word!) of verse 7.

    a.   Psalm 56:8 is three lines: one beautiful statement developed by two pictures. Muse on this verse and these pictures. What do they make you see and understand about God?

    b.   Psalm 56:9 is three lines that culminate in a remarkable claim. To grasp how David could dare to make this claim, recall that promise we read in 2 Samuel 7:12–17. How can we make this claim as well? Read Romans 8:31–34.

    c.   Psalm 56:10–11 brings the refrain we heard in verse 4, but with an added line. What is the effect of finding this refrain at this point and with these added words?

4. Oh, what a marvelous conclusion to this psalm!

    a. Consider the central pair of parallel lines in Psalm 56:12–13. Write your thoughts about just what action it is that gives the psalmist his confidence here. How does the whole Bible reveal this action?

    b. The psalmist is released to do *what*, with *whom*, here at the end? What's the final picture, and why does it make such a good conclusion to this whole psalm?

5. In what ways does this psalm comfort you, challenge you, or teach you? How might it lead you to pray?

DAY FOUR—DIG IN YOURSELF (PSALM 57)

Psalm 57 brings another cry for deliverance and another answer to that cry. Consider the following questions and notes.

1. Upon prayerful reading and rereading, what initial <u>observations</u> would you make?

2. Who wrote this psalm, and how much do we know about the <u>context</u>? (See 1 Samuel 22:1–2; 24:1–7.)

3. What <u>shape</u> does this psalm have? *Note the beginning and ending, the progression of sections, and patterns and repetitions of words and ideas. How wonderful to find here another refrain—how does it help delineate the sections?*

4. Does a <u>main idea</u> begin to emerge? *Note: Keep coming back to this question as you make your way through the others.*

5. How do the <u>parallel lines</u> and the <u>imagery</u> communicate in this poem? *Note: In each psalm, different elements will stand out. Do take time to see and muse on the vivid imagery in Psalm 57. One exercise would be to picture every different place in which the psalmist pictures himself.*

6. In what ways does this psalm point us to <u>Christ</u>? *Note: Sometimes a cluster of theologically rich words emerges, as in this psalm—words about God's mercy, his purpose, his saving, and his steadfast love and faithfulness. We will meet often the words stead-*fast love, *sometimes translated "unfailing love" or "lovingkindness" from the Hebrew* hesed, *often referring to God's covenant love for his people. To what must all these words ultimately point?*

7. What sorts of personal <u>applications and prayers</u> might you take away from this psalm?

(Continued from previous page)

DAY FIVE—TAKE IT IN

Reread the two psalms you have studied in this lesson, and from them choose a verse or passage you would like to memorize. Write out the verse or passage and commit it to memory (or begin to do so!). Make these words a part of your thinking and your prayers. Be ready, if you wish, to share with your group why you chose these words and how they are working in your heart.

Thoughts and Observations—Psalm 51

Lesson 5
(Psalms 51 & 130)

THE WAY OF REPENTANCE

The Psalms show us the ways of God, and by contrast they help us see our own sinful ways. A number of "penitential psalms" lead us in humble repentance before God, offering beautiful models of coming before him to ask for his forgiveness. Both psalms for this week help us learn to come with repentant hearts before the Lord God.

DAY ONE—READ AND OBSERVE

- To begin, pray—thanking God for these inspired words and asking to understand them. You might use Scripture from Psalm 119 or from other psalms you've been reading.

- Read through Psalm 51 without pause, taking it in as a whole.

- Reread it several times, stopping to think and observe and marking words and sections that stand out to you.

- Finally, write down (on page 56) at least five initial observations concerning the words you read in this psalm. They can be the most basic sorts of observations. What do you notice? What stands out to you in this psalm?

DAY TWO—GETTING THE IDEA

1. Psalm 51 grew out of vivid personal experience. Read 2 Samuel 11:1–12:15. What can you observe about David's repentance in that passage? What connections do you find with Psalm 51?

2. How would you divide this psalm into sections, and how would you title and briefly explain each one?

3. What train of thought moves through this poem from beginning to end? What connecting words help make the logic clear? Can you put the logical flow of the psalm into one sentence?

4. Find and comment on key words and key patterns of words in this psalm. For example, in Psalm 51:1–2, what key words establish the basis on which the psalmist approaches God? What three words together define his problem and what three words together express what he asks God to do about it? What is the effect of these clusters of words?

5. What is this psalm mainly about? How would you state the main idea of Psalm 51?

DAY THREE—FILLING IN THE PICTURE

1. The initial statement in Psalm 51:1–2 is offered to a God who had revealed himself to David and his people and continued to do so through the prophets. Comment on how the following verses shed light on the opening of Psalm 51.

   a. Exodus 34:4–9

   b. Numbers 19:1–10

c. Isaiah 1:4, 15–18 (Note here the pictures in common with Psalm 51 and the vivid effect of these pictures.)

2. Rather than simply saying, "I have sinned," the psalmist teaches us in profound ways what that means, even as he speaks personally to God. In what ways does each set of parallel lines in Psalm 51:3–6 teach us something important about our sin?

3. Each pair of lines in Psalm 51:7–12 works together beautifully so that the passage offers six requests of God. Comment on *what* and *how* the psalmist asks in each one. (Don't forget to take time for the pictures.)

4. Psalm 51:13–19 broadens out to the poem's end.

   a. What various results of repentance can you observe in these verses?

b. What various truths about God can we learn in these verses? (How wonderful and instructive that we should end this prayer looking not inward but upward!)

5. Consider the ways in which this very personal prayer of repentance is given to God's people in all times and places—including ours.

a. First, we can't leave the psalm without looking to the Bible's full revelation about how this cleansing happens completely and finally. Read Hebrews 10:1–22 and summarize that passage's good news of cleansing.

b. Look back through Psalm 51. How might this psalm affect your thinking, your prayers, your worship, and your relationship with God?

Day Four—Dig In Yourself (Psalm 130)

We're jumping ahead to the "psalms of ascent" toward the end of the book—those psalms associated with the procession of Jewish worshipers up toward the temple in Jerusalem, the city built on Mount Zion. Included in that group is this remarkable little psalm of penitence and of hope. You'll notice some of the same key words you saw in Psalm 51. Consider the following questions and notes for Psalm 130.

1. Upon prayerful reading and rereading, what initial observations would you make?

2. Consider the context of the psalms of ascent. How might Psalm 130 be appropriate for a group of worshipers approaching the temple?

3. What shape does this psalm have? *Note the beginning and ending, the progression of sections, and patterns and repetitions of words and ideas.*

4. Does a <u>main idea</u> begin to emerge? *Note: Keep coming back to this question as you make your way through the others.*

5. How do the <u>parallel lines</u> and the <u>imagery</u> communicate in this poem? *Note: In each psalm, different elements will stand out. There is one striking, repeated picture in this poem. Why is it repeated? What does the picture communicate, particularly in the progression of this poem and in relation to its main idea?*

6. In what ways does this psalm point us to <u>Christ</u>? *Note: We have seen how sometimes a cluster of theologically rich words emerges—and in that cluster is often found the Hebrew word* hesed *(translated "steadfast love," "unfailing love," "lovingkindness"). What rich words in Psalm 130:7–8 point to the Bible's ultimate hope?*

7. What sorts of personal <u>applications and prayers</u> might you take away from this psalm?

(Continued from previous page)

Day Five—Take It In

Reread the two psalms you have studied in this lesson, and from them choose a verse or passage you would like to memorize. Write out the verse or passage and commit it to memory (or begin to do so!). Make these words a part of your thinking and your prayers. Be ready, if you wish, to share with your group why you chose these words and how they are working in your heart.

Thoughts and Observations—Psalm 66

Lesson 6 (Psalms 66 & 67)
THE WAY OF LARGE PRAISE

We are seeing that the Psalms speak to our personal experience—and so much more! The two psalms for this week again touch us as individuals, but they also reach out in space and time to encompass the breadth of God's redemptive plan. May these psalms stretch our hearts.

DAY ONE—READ AND OBSERVE

- To begin, pray—thanking God for these inspired words and asking to understand them. You might use Scripture from Psalm 119 or from other psalms you've been reading.

- Read through Psalm 66 without pause, taking it in as a whole.

- Reread it several times, stopping to think and observe and marking words and sections that stand out to you.

- Finally, write down (on the facing page) at least five initial observations concerning the words you read

in this psalm. They can be the most basic sorts of observations. What do you notice? What stands out to you in this psalm?

DAY TWO—GETTING THE IDEA

1. This psalm doesn't give the context of an author. However, this might be one of the several sequences in the Psalms that evidence an intended logical order. Glancing back at Psalm 65, especially its final verse, how would you say Psalm 66 logically follows Psalm 65? *Note: "All the earth" in Psalm 66 embraces all the people of the earth.*

2. Divide Psalm 66 into sections, suggesting your own title and brief description of each.

3. Now analyze the flow of all these sections. What is the shape of this psalm, from beginning to end? *Note: How might you draw it?*

4. Trace and comment on the patterns and repetitions of words and phrases you find in Psalm 66. *Note: For this psalm, it is helpful to trace the idea of giving voice to prayer and praise—to a God who hears.*

5. What is this psalm mainly about? How would you state the main idea of Psalm 66?

Day Three—Filling In the Picture

1. In Psalm 66:1–4, the psalmist gives an intricately patterned opening call! What's at the center, in verse 3, and what encases the center, on either side? Relish the beauty of these verses in every way you can.

2. In Psalm 66:5–12, the psalm focuses in, in layers.

   a. In Psalm 66:5–7, what act of God is at the center, and what larger focus encases it?

   b. From Psalm 66:1–8, list all the words relating to this larger, worldwide focus. How might Psalm 2 and Genesis 12:1–3 illumine these words?

c. In Psalm 66:8–12, what's the logical flow of
    thought? (Notice the transition words that intro-
    duce verse 10 and the last line of verse 12.)

d. How are those pictures in Psalm 66:10–12 vivid and
    effective in communicating all kinds of suffering
    endured by God's people even today?

3. If someone asked you to explain the importance and
    appropriateness of verses 13–20 in the whole of Psalm
    66, what might you say?

4. Psalm 66:13–15 refers to burnt offerings, offerings that were not partly eaten and enjoyed by the community but rather entirely consumed by fire, showing complete dedication, utter consecration to the Lord. Psalm 66:16–19 explains the reason for such intent worship.

   a. Apart from whatever deliverance is referred to, what is it about God that overwhelms the psalmist in Psalm 66:16–19? What phrases stand out, and why?

   b. Psalm 66:18 has to do with the motivations of our hearts. What can we learn (and not learn) here? And how does Psalm 66:19 immediately emphasize the merciful truth at the heart of it all?

c. The Old Testament worshipers put their faith in God's promises to hear and purify and deliver his people. Stop, consider, and thank God for the promised one through whom God hears and purifies and delivers us. Thank God that the deliverer came and that we know his name and can tell what he has done for our souls. Stop to think on Jesus. Pray that our worship in his name would become a testimony throughout *all the earth!*

5. Psalm 66:20 gives us the psalmist's response—and helps us with ours! What aspects of God's *hesed*, God's "steadfast love," have been evident in this psalm? How do you respond?

Day Four—Dig In Yourself (Psalm 67)

In Psalm 67 we find the same wonderful juxtaposition of close-up and worldwide perspectives. These psalms touch our hearts personally and also stretch them to see God's plan for the nations of the world. Consider the following questions and notes.

1. Upon prayerful reading and rereading, what initial <u>observations</u> would you make?

2. Consider the <u>context</u> of Psalm 67. For the broader biblical context, read Numbers 6:22–27 and Genesis 12:1–3.

3. What <u>shape</u> does this psalm have? *Note the beginning and ending—particularly, in this psalm, the matching "bookends" of the first two and the last two verses. Then find the "bookends" encasing the middle section. What's at the center? Note also patterns of words—for example, all the words that stretch our vision far.*

4. Does a <u>main idea</u> begin to emerge? *Note: Keep coming back to this question as you make your way through the others.*

5. How do the <u>parallel lines</u> and the <u>imagery</u> communicate in this poem? *Note: In each psalm, different elements will stand out. In relation to imagery, what is that harvest picture doing there toward the end?*

6. In what ways does this psalm point us to <u>Christ</u>? *Consider: How did God accomplish his promise to Abraham that through his seed all the nations of the earth would be blessed? How does this perspective open up this psalm for us now, at our point in salvation history?*

7. What sorts of personal <u>applications and prayers</u> might you take away from this psalm? *Note: How might this psalm have a transformative effect on our prayer life?*

(Continued from previous page)

(Continued from previous page)

Day Five—Take It In

Reread the two psalms you have studied in this lesson, and from them choose a verse or passage you would like to memorize. Write out the verse or passage and commit it to memory (or begin to do so!). Make these words a part of your thinking and your prayers. Be ready, if you wish, to share with your group why you chose these words and how they are working in your heart.

Thoughts and Observations—Psalm 85

Lesson 7 (Psalms 85 & 126)

THE WAY BETWEEN
ALREADY AND NOT YET

God's people know what it's like to live while looking both *backward* (to the marvelous acts of God) and *forward* (to further deliverance and blessing to come). We saw in Psalm 66 the way the exodus from Egypt loomed large as the great picture of God's past deliverance. In Psalm 2 we encountered God's promise of deliverance and perfect justice through a great King in the line of David.

From the perspective of our own time, we look back and celebrate the coming of King Jesus, who on the cross delivered us from the ultimate bondage to sin and death. We also look forward, to Jesus' coming again and to the consummation of the salvation story. Along with God's people in past centuries, we understand these psalms that show us the way between the "already" and the "not yet."

DAY ONE—READ AND OBSERVE

- To begin, pray—thanking God for these inspired words and asking to understand them. You might use Scripture from Psalm 119 or from other psalms you've been reading.

- Read through Psalm 85 without pause, taking it in as a whole.

- Reread it several times, stopping to think and observe and marking words and sections that stand out to you.

- Finally, write down (on page 80) at least five initial observations concerning the words you read in this psalm. They can be the most basic sorts of observations. What do you notice? What stands out to you in this psalm?

Day Two—Getting the Idea

1. The context of Psalm 85 is not explicit. Some think it was composed long after King David, long after the kingdom had split and fallen, after the people had been taken into exile but then finally allowed by Persian king Cyrus to return to their land. Those exiles were thankful to return but were quickly discouraged by the huge task of rebuilding a devastated land and a broken-down Jerusalem. But that's just one example of the kind of context out of which this psalm might have grown. What clues to its context do you find in the psalm itself?

2. What about the shape of Psalm 85? Divide this psalm into four sections, suggesting your own title and brief description of each.

3. Consider the development of the poem from beginning to end. How does each section flow logically into the next? Why is each section crucial?

4. What words in Psalm 85 echo words in Exodus 34:4–9? What patterns and repetitions of these words do you find in the psalm?

5. What is this psalm mainly about? How would you state the main idea of Psalm 85?

Day Three—Filling In the Picture

1. Study the progression of verbs (the things God *did*) in the lines of Psalm 85:1–3. How do verses 2–3 develop the meaning of verse 1 in significant and perhaps even unexpected ways?

2. In what ways does the meaning of Psalm 85:1–3 help us understand what the psalmist is asking for in Psalm 85:4–7? How do those wonderful, weighty words in Psalm 85:7 sum up all that we could ever ask from God?

3. This psalm just gets more and more beautiful. Read and think on Psalm 85:8–9.

   a. What parts of these verses help us understand and even picture God's close presence with his people?

   b. What kinds of responses to God are modeled and urged in these verses? (See also Habakkuk 2:1.)

    c.   What echoes do you find in Zechariah 9:9–10 and John 1:14? Explain in your own words the way in which Jesus Christ shines through Psalm 85:8–9 in light of the full context of Scripture.

4. In Psalm 85:10–13, an amazing climax develops as the psalmist pictures various kinds of unions, or meetings.

    a.   List and comment on the various meetings you find in these verses.

b. How might these various meetings all find their final meaning in Jesus' death for us on the cross? (For context, read Romans 3:21–26; 5:1–2.)

c. Psalm 85:12–13 closes with statements of confidence about the future. How does the whole psalm help us understand what this confidence is all about? (And what is the effect of that final verse? Why does the psalm end the way it does?)

5. In what ways do you think the church now can identify with this psalm? In what ways does this psalm challenge and encourage you?

Day Four—Dig In Yourself (Psalm 126)

Psalm 126 (another one of the psalms of ascent) shares the same rhythm of looking both back and ahead that we saw in Psalm 85. Consider the following questions and notes.

1. Upon prayerful reading and rereading, what initial <u>observations</u> would you make?

2. Consider the <u>context</u> of Psalm 126. Although the context is not specifically clear, how might this psalm, like Psalm 85, seem to refer to the returned exiles? *Consider: what is the effect of having the context be somewhat vague and general?*

3. What <u>shape</u> does this psalm have? *Note the beginning and ending, the discernible sections, and patterns and repetitions of words and ideas.*

4. Does a <u>main idea</u> begin to emerge? *Note: Keep coming back to this question as you make your way through the others.*

5. How do the <u>parallel lines</u> and the <u>imagery</u> communicate in this poem? *Note: In each psalm, different elements will stand out. This psalm's pictures are powerful; take time to see them and muse on them.*

6. In what ways does this psalm point us to <u>Christ</u>? *Note: This psalm has fewer direct references and more general ones. In light of all Scripture, how is final restoration accomplished? One might trace that picture of the harvest forward to a scene like that of John 4:27–42.*

7. What sorts of personal <u>applications and prayers</u> might you take away from this psalm? *Note: How might this psalm help us to pray—not only for ourselves, but for the promised harvest?*

(Continued from previous page)

Day Five—Take It In

Reread the two psalms you have studied in this lesson, and from them choose a verse or passage you would like to memorize. Write out the verse or passage and commit it to memory (or begin to do so!). Make these words a part of your thinking and your prayers. Be ready, if you wish, to share with your group why you chose these words and how they are working in your heart.

Thoughts and Observations—Psalm 86

Lesson 8 (Psalms 86 & 138)
THE WAY OF
TRUSTING IN TROUBLE

Some psalms focus on *deliverance* from trouble. In the two psalms for this week, David speaks words of faith out of the midst of ongoing trouble. We need these psalms—and how they minister to us in the midst of ongoing life!

DAY ONE—READ AND OBSERVE

- To begin, pray—thanking God for these inspired words and asking to understand them. You might use Scripture from Psalm 119 or from other psalms you've been reading.

- Read through Psalm 86 without pause, taking it in as a whole.

- Reread it several times, stopping to think and observe and marking words and sections that stand out to you.

- Finally, write down (on the facing page) at least five initial observations concerning the words you read

in this psalm. They can be the most basic sorts of observations. What do you notice? What stands out to you in this psalm?

Day Two—Getting the Idea

1. Psalm 86 is the only psalm by David in the third book of the Psalms. Although again the context is not specifically clear, what facts can we discern from the psalm about the situation in which David writes these words?

2. This psalm (like many) could be divided up in a number of different ways. One possibility might be to find a central section and work from there. Study the psalm's shape, divide it up into sections, and give each section your own title and brief description.

3. Trace and comment on the patterns and repetitions of words and phrases you find in this psalm. You might look for patterns of petitions ("incline," "answer," "preserve," etc.), or patterns of logical connectors (like "for" and "but"), or other patterns as well.

4. Find in Psalm 86 echoes of that passage we've already seen echoed in the Psalms: Exodus 34:4–9. By now you are noticing and probably coming to relish the beautiful Old Testament Hebrew word *hesed*—God's *steadfast love*, his unfailing lovingkindness toward his people. How is the truth of Exodus 34:4–9 (and especially the truth of God's *hesed*) key to understanding Psalm 86?

5. What is this psalm mainly about? How would you state the main idea of Psalm 86?

DAY THREE—FILLING IN THE PICTURE

1. In Psalm 86, David offers God many reasons why God should answer his prayers.

   a. From Psalm 86:1–4, list all the different reasons that relate to *himself. Note: David's claim to be "godly" in verse 2 can be best interpreted by the parallel line of that verse and by the context of the whole psalm.*

   b. What makes these reasons in Psalm 86:1–4 "godly"? *Consider other reasons we might be tempted to offer to God or other heart motives that might direct similar words. Consider as well the relationship and the knowledge these words reflect.*

c.   The reasons quickly grow into a full focus on God. On what qualities of God does David stake his prayer in Psalm 86:5–7?

2. Psalm 86:8–10 stands out as this psalm's strong, central affirmation about God.

a.   Examine and comment on the shape of these three verses: what similar affirmations do verses 8 and 10 both make—and what happens in the middle? *Note: "among the gods" may refer to angelic beings or to false gods of other nations.*

    b. How might Psalm 86:9 take us back to Genesis 12:1–3, back to Psalm 2, and ahead to Revelation 7:9–12; 15:4?

3. In what ways does Psalm 86:11–13 offer a response to verses 8–10? Comment especially on the psalmist's words about his heart and his soul.

4. Consider the way Psalm 86 draws to a close.

    a. Why do you think David's specific mention of his circumstances does not come until the final verses (Ps. 86:14–17)?

b. How does Psalm 86:14–17 evidence the same perspective and approach we have seen from the psalm's beginning (vv. 1–4)?

5. Which of David's requests of God in this psalm would you like to learn to pray more effectively in the midst of trouble? Why? According to this psalm, *how*?

Day Four—Dig In Yourself (Psalm 138)

As in Psalm 86, David in Psalm 138 speaks "in the midst of trouble" (Ps. 138:7). How comforting that the Bible acknowledges this place! Consider the following questions and notes.

1. Upon prayerful reading and rereading, what initial observations would you make?

2. Consider the context of Psalm 138. *Note: There is no specific historical context; simply discern everything you can from the text about the situation in which David speaks—and then marvel at the tone and main idea.*

3. What shape does this psalm have? *Note the beginning and ending, the discernible sections, and patterns and repetitions of words and ideas. Do notice the recurring "steadfast love" that enfolds this psalm. What happens in the middle of the psalm?*

4. Does a main idea begin to emerge? *Note: Keep coming back to this question as you make your way through the others.*

5. How do the parallel lines and the imagery communicate in this poem? *Note: In each psalm, different elements will stand out. Psalm 138 is full of details of God's mercy personally directed toward his children, as we contemplate his hearing and speaking to us, his seeing us, his reaching out his hand. . . .*

6. In what ways does this psalm point us to Christ? *Note: Psalm 138:4–6 might take us to the same passages we read in connection with Psalm 86:8–10. We also might look back to the promise of 2 Samuel 7:12–17 in connection with Psalm 138:8. What was God's promised purpose for David, and how was that purpose fulfilled? What does that have to do with God's purpose for each of his children?*

7. What sorts of personal applications and prayers might you take away from this psalm?

(Continued from previous page)

(Continued from previous page)

DAY FIVE—TAKE IT IN

Reread the two psalms you have studied in this lesson, and from them choose a verse or passage you would like to memorize. Write out the verse or passage and commit it to memory (or begin to do so!). Make these words a part of your thinking and your prayers. Be ready, if you wish, to share with your group why you chose these words and how they are working in your heart.

Thoughts and Observations—Psalm 92

Lesson 9 (Psalms 92 & 93)

THE WAY OF PRAISE TO GOD ON HIGH

These two psalms have a focus: God himself. These words refresh our souls as we look up and give him praise.

DAY ONE—READ AND OBSERVE

- To begin, pray—thanking God for these inspired words and asking to understand them. You might use Scripture from Psalm 119 or from other psalms you've been reading.

- Read through Psalm 92 without pause, taking it in as a whole.

- Reread it several times, stopping to think and observe and marking words and sections that stand out to you.

- Finally, write down (on the facing page) at least five initial observations concerning the words you read in this psalm. They can be the most basic sorts of observations. What do you notice? What stands out to you in this psalm?

DAY TWO—GETTING THE IDEA

1. The author of Psalm 92 is not named, but the main context is clear and beautiful: this is the only psalm written for the Sabbath (see Ex. 20:8–11; Lev. 23:1–3; Deut. 5:12–15). How does the content of the psalm seem to fit its designated occasion?

2. Psalm 92 has been divided a number of different ways. How might you divide this psalm into sections? Offer a title and brief description of each section.

3. Psalm 92 does not have many obvious patterns or repetitions of words and phrases moving throughout the whole psalm. One pattern, however, relates to high and low. What words in this psalm refer to heights and depths? How might these words relate to the main idea or even the shape of the psalm?

4. How would you explain the logical progression of thought in Psalm 92, section by section from beginning to end? *Note the repeated word that helps make the transition between verse 4 and verse 5.*

5. What is this psalm mainly about? How would you state the main idea of Psalm 92?

Day Three—Filling In the Picture

1. Psalm 92:1–4 ushers us right into a worship gathering! Describe what you hear, think, and feel in the process of these verses. Comments?

2. With Psalm 92:5, the psalmist steps back from the immediate experience of one day's worship to think on the eternal truths he is blessed to know—in contrast with those who "cannot know" (v. 6).

a.   Summarize what it is that the "fool," or "stupid man," cannot know or understand (Ps. 92:5–9).

b.   Psalm 92:7–9 is amazingly patterned. Write down your observations about these verses, considering questions such as: How does Psalm 92:8 make a central point in relation to the three lines on either side? What repetitions of words or phrases do you notice just within verses 7–9, and what is the effect?

c.   With the "but" that begins Psalm 92:10–11, the psalmist contrasts himself with these enemies of God. How do these verses bring vivid meaning—and stark contrast—to the previous verses? *Note: The "wild ox" was a strong beast that could gore its enemies with its tusks.*

> *"Fresh oil" brings to mind the oil of consecration for sacrifice, or perhaps oil of refreshment and healing, or perhaps even the oil of anointing.*

3. Psalm 92 ends with a picture of ongoing worship!

   a. Who are the "righteous" of Psalm 92:12 in the context of this whole psalm? (Notice even the psalm's final verse.)

   b. Notice the word "flourish" twice in Psalm 92:12–15. In what previous verse did this word occur also, and how does the picture of that verse contrast with the pictures developed in this last section? What do these rich final pictures communicate?

c.   What about that picture in the psalm's final verse? How does Psalm 92:15 draw this whole psalm to a beautiful and appropriate conclusion?

4. The New Testament book of Hebrews talks about a "Sabbath rest for the people of God" (Heb. 4:9)—referring to the rest of salvation brought about not by our own works but by the work of Jesus on the cross to redeem us from our sin and make us his righteous people. How amazing to be called to Sabbath worship by Psalm 92 and to know the Christ who is "lord of the Sabbath" (Matt. 12:8). Reread this psalm in light of Jesus' death and resurrection, which conquered sin and death forever. Then, to close this day's study, write your thoughts in personal response to this psalm.

DAY FOUR—DIG IN YOURSELF (PSALM 93)

Psalm 93 begins a progression of "royal psalms," psalms focusing on the King! This psalm turns our eyes immediately and vividly to the King of heaven. Consider the following questions and notes.

1. Upon prayerful reading and rereading, what initial observations would you make?

2. Consider the context of Psalm 93. *Note: There is no clear context! Why is that actually helpful?*

3. What shape does this psalm have? *Note the beginning and ending, the discernible sections, and patterns and repetitions of words and ideas. The repetitions in this poem are actually part of the way the poetry works, as a line repeats something but adds on to the meaning, thereby growing or emphasizing that meaning right in front of our eyes. In Hebrew, to emphasize a word you don't put "very" before it; you say it twice—or three times! This comment of course applies to question 5 as well.*

4. Does a main idea begin to emerge? *Note: Keep coming back to this question as you make your way through the others.*

5. How do the parallel lines and the imagery communicate in this poem? *Note: In each psalm, different elements will stand out. This powerful progression of lines brings a vivid series of pictures. Note that the sea, in Hebrew thinking, usually represents threatening chaos and evil.*

6. In what ways does this psalm point us to Christ? *Note: We've begun to open the store of verses that show us the Christ who reigns. Which of the ones we've seen might connect most directly with this psalm? There are many others that exalt the everlasting King Jesus—for example, 1 Timothy 6:14–16.*

7. What sorts of personal applications and prayers might you take away from this psalm? *Note: What difference does the Lord who reigns make to your life today? To your prayers? To your study of his Word?*

(Continued from previous page)

(Continued from previous page)

DAY FIVE—TAKE IT IN

Reread the two psalms you have studied in this lesson, and from them choose a verse or passage you would like to memorize. Write out the verse or passage and commit it to memory (or begin to do so!). Make these words a part of your thinking and your prayers. Be ready, if you wish, to share with your group why you chose these words and how they are working in your heart.

Thoughts and Observations—Psalm 81

Lesson 10 (Psalms 81 & 95)
THE WAY OF EXHORTATION

Psalm 81 and Psalm 95 both call us to worship, but with sober warnings—warnings that look back to the hard hearts of the Israelites in the wilderness. These psalms call God's people to be instructed by those examples, that we might listen to the Lord, walk in his ways, and worship him truly.

DAY ONE—READ AND OBSERVE

- To begin, pray—thanking God for these inspired words and asking to understand them. You might use Scripture from Psalm 119 or from other psalms you've been reading.

- Read through Psalm 81 without pause, taking it in as a whole.

- Reread it several times, stopping to think and observe and marking words and sections that stand out to you.

- Finally, write down (on the facing page) at least five initial observations concerning the words you read

in this psalm. They can be the most basic sorts of observations. What do you notice? What stands out to you in this psalm?

DAY TWO—GETTING THE IDEA

1. This psalm has especially deep layers of historical context.

   a. First, simply read Psalm 81:1–3, along with the descriptions of the feasts it may have been written to celebrate in Leviticus 23:23–44.

   b. Psalm 81:4–10 refers to God's judgment on the Egyptians and his deliverance of his people from slavery (Ex. 12), the people's lack of trust in God at Meribah (Ex. 17:1–7; Num. 20:1–13), and the giving of the law at Mount Sinai (Ex. 19–20). Simply look through these several related passages as background crucial to Psalm 81.

   c. The whole of Psalm 81, including the final section (vv. 11–16), recalls the themes and words of the Song of Moses, which he gave to the Israelites before his death. Read part of this song, in Deuteronomy 32:1–18, and note the echoes you find in Psalm 81.

2. Three main sections of Psalm 81 emerge. Suggest a title and brief description for each of these sections.

3. Consider how these sections fit together. How does the public worship to which we're joyfully called in the first section fit with (or not fit with) the things talked about in the other sections? What are those things?

4. What is this psalm mainly about? How would you state the main idea of Psalm 81?

Day Three—Filling In the Picture

1. List all the sounds of Psalm 81:1–3. What do you hear and picture?

2. The rest of the psalm has a different sound, one introduced in Psalm 81:4–5 and continuing basically through the rest of the psalm. What is this other sound (and of whose voice, starting in verse 5?), and how would you describe its tone? What words and phrases from the text explain your answer?

3. God's Word, God's own voice, stands out in this poem. Even the worship called for at the start is worship decreed by God in his Law.

   a. Write down all the references in this psalm to God's speaking and our listening.

   b. How might God's offer to *feed* us fit into this same theme? How does this picture work? (Read Deuteronomy 8:1–3.)

c.   God's words come with actions; words and works go together. Our listening to his words must be accompanied by what? Consider the way the parallel lines work in Psalm 81:11, 13.

4. It would be misleading to take this psalm as simply a warning all about us. The psalm focuses not on our perspective but on God's! Consider the nature of this psalm's exhortation.

a.   According to Psalm 81:11–15, how does God view and treat those who do not listen to his voice? See also Romans 1:18–32.

b.   How might you logically expect the second section (Ps. 81:8–10) and the third section (vv. 11–16) to end? What is wonderful and surprising about the way they do indeed end?

c. How might we sum up this psalm's exhortation as closely as possible to the way the psalm delivers it?

5. Consider the implications of this psalm for those of us who know the Lord Jesus Christ.

    a. First, read 1 Corinthians 10:1–13 and John 6:25–40. Jot down words or phrases that stand out.

b. How do you respond? How might Psalm 81 encourage and exhort you as you worship regularly with Christ's body and live in relationship with this God who actually speaks to us through his Word?

DAY FOUR—DIG IN YOURSELF (PSALM 95)

Psalm 95 again calls us to sing joyfully—and again turns to sober exhortation. Consider the following questions and notes.

1. Upon prayerful reading and rereading, what initial <u>observations</u> would you make?

2. Consider the <u>context</u> of Psalm 95. *Note: In what ways is the context of this psalm similar to and different from that of Psalm 81?*

3. What <u>shape</u> does this psalm have? *Note the beginning and ending, the discernible sections, and patterns and repetitions of words and ideas. What an ending this psalm has! Why do you think it ends this way?*

4. Does a <u>main idea</u> begin to emerge? *Note: Keep coming back to this question as you make your way through the others.*

5. How do the <u>parallel lines</u> and the <u>imagery</u> communicate in this poem? *Note: In each psalm, different elements will stand out. Through what vivid pictures does this psalm tell us who is the God we worship?*

6. In what ways does this psalm point us to <u>Christ</u>? *Note: Read John 10:14 and Hebrews 3:1–4:13.*

7. What sorts of personal <u>applications and prayers</u> might you take away from this psalm?

(Continued from previous page)

Day Five—Take It In

Reread the two psalms you have studied in this lesson, and from them choose a verse or passage you would like to memorize. Write out the verse or passage and commit it to memory (or begin to do so!). Make these words a part of your thinking and your prayers. Be ready, if you wish, to share with your group why you chose these words and how they are working in your heart.

Thoughts and Observations—Psalm 102

Lesson 11
(Psalms 102 & 94)

THE WAY OF
FARSIGHTED LAMENT

These two psalms emerge from great affliction. In the midst of that affliction comes vision—farsighted, God-centered vision. These psalms help God's people remember that our earthly lives are part of a huge redemptive story with an assured and unfathomably good resolution.

DAY ONE—READ AND OBSERVE

- To begin, pray—thanking God for these inspired words and asking to understand them. You might use Scripture from Psalm 119 or from other psalms you've been reading.

- Read through Psalm 102 without pause, taking it in as a whole.

- Reread it several times, stopping to think and observe and marking words and sections that stand out to you.

- Finally, write down (on page 128) at least five initial observations concerning the words you read in this psalm. They can be the most basic sorts of observations. What do you notice? What stands out to you in this psalm?

DAY TWO—GETTING THE IDEA

1. The heading of Psalm 102 is rather general but quite vivid! What can you tell from it and from the whole psalm about the context in which it was written?

2. How would you divide Psalm 102 into sections? Clearly there's at least one turning point, in verse 12. Suggest a title and brief description for each of your sections.

3. Consider the shape of this poem.

    a.   Contrast Psalm 102:1–2 (how do these verses communicate such urgency?) with verse 28. Make as many observations as possible about the differences you notice.

    b.   What contrasts do you notice between the two sides of that turning point in Psalm 102:12—both directly on either side, and in the poem as a whole? Consider, for example, contrasts in focus on persons, time, and place. (What repeated words help indicate the differing focus on time?)

c.   How do both sides of that turning point acknowledge the sovereign hand of God—but do so differently?

4. The covenant promises of God to Abraham (Gen. 12:1–3) and David (2 Sam. 7:12–17) loom large in this poem. What parts of Psalm 102 especially reveal the psalmist's hope in these promises?

5. What is this psalm mainly about? How would you state the main idea of Psalm 102?

Day Three—Filling In the Picture

1. What powerful imagery is in this poem! From Psalm 102:3–11, list and muse on all the pictures the psalmist uses to communicate his plight. Write your thoughts on what sorts of images these are and how they communicate so effectively.

2. Consider what we learn of God in this psalm.

   a. We don't really look at him until that turning point. How is God presented and pictured in Psalm 102:12–24? What qualities of God clearly emerge in these verses?

   b. Psalm 102:25–28 concludes the psalm with a remarkable statement of who God is—stretching the perspective of time far in both directions. Consider the picture here and the truths presented. What do you see, and what do you learn?

    c.   Read Hebrews 1 to find Psalm 102:25-27 quoted. What main point is the writer of Hebrews making? In that light, how does Psalm 102 stretch our understanding of God?

3. The point of this psalm is clear in Psalm 102:18–22. *Note: Zion, or Jerusalem, indicates not just a physical city but the spiritual reality of God's dwelling with his people—as in Isaiah 2:1–3 and Hebrews 11:8–16.*

    a.   According to Psalm 102:18, what does the psalmist want to see happen as the result of this psalm?

    b.   The two lines of Psalm 102:18 are explained by verses 19–20 and verses 21–22. How?

   c. How do *we* fit into these verses as believers in Jesus Christ, who came to set us free from sin and death?

4. Psalm 102 does not leave behind the reality of the psalmist's suffering. How does the psalm continue to acknowledge it—and what does it do with it? What can we learn from this whole psalm in the midst of suffering today?

Day Four—Dig In Yourself (Psalm 94)

We come to another psalm full of anguished questions that can be answered only with farsighted, God-centered vision. Consider the following questions and notes for Psalm 94.

1. Upon prayerful reading and rereading, what initial <u>observations</u> would you make?

2. Consider the <u>context</u> of Psalm 94. *Note: Here's another psalm with no specific context—and extremely broad possibilities of*

application. Consider the context of the psalm's ideas from passages like Deuteronomy 32:34–42.

3. What <u>shape</u> does this psalm have? *Note the beginning and ending, the discernible sections, and patterns and repetitions of words and ideas.*

4. Does a <u>main idea</u> begin to emerge? *Note: Keep coming back to this question as you make your way through the others.*

5. How do the <u>parallel lines</u> and the <u>imagery</u> communicate in this poem? *Note: In each psalm, different elements will stand out. Consider the dramatic effect of the first flow of lines that build up the problem addressed—and then the dramatic effect of those questions piled up in verses 8–11. Watch for familiar pictures of the temporary span of earthly life in contrast with the stability of the Lord himself.*

6. In what ways does this psalm point us to <u>Christ</u>? *Note: It's helpful to remember that the concept of God's vengeance in this psalm is not simply an Old Testament concept. Consider, for example, 2 Thessalonians 1:5–12, which rather directly connects this concept to Christ Jesus himself.*

7. What sorts of personal <u>applications and prayers</u> might you take away from this psalm?

(*Continued from previous page*)

(Continued from previous page)

Day Five—Take It In

Reread the two psalms you have studied in this lesson, and from them choose a verse or passage you would like to memorize. Write out the verse or passage and commit it to memory (or begin to do so!). Make these words a part of your thinking and your prayers. Be ready, if you wish, to share with your group why you chose these words and how they are working in your heart.

Thoughts and Observations—Psalm 147

Lesson 12
(Psalms 147 & 148)
THE WAY THROUGH
GOD'S WORLD

We conclude by looking at two psalms that offer praise to our God, who not only saves his people but rules over and provides for all his creation. These psalms offer one more example of the way the whole book of Psalms enlarges our understanding and our worship of the Lord God. May we be encouraged to keep coming back to the Psalms, again and again, and to follow them into ever deeper worship and praise.

DAY ONE—READ AND OBSERVE

- To begin, pray—thanking God for these inspired words and asking to understand them. You might use Scripture from Psalm 119 or from other psalms you've been reading.

- Read through Psalm 147 without pause, taking it in as a whole.

- Reread it several times, stopping to think and observe and marking words and sections that stand out to you.

- Finally, write down (on page 140) at least five initial observations concerning the words you read in this psalm. They can be the most basic sorts of observations. What do you notice? What stands out to you in this psalm?

Day Two—Getting the Idea

1. Psalm 147 is another without a specific context, but in it we can see clearly the people for whom and from whom it comes.

   a. In what various ways are those people referred to in this psalm?

   b. Many have suggested that this psalm might have been written to celebrate the release of the Jewish exiles from their captivity, as they returned to Jerusalem and rebuilt their ravaged city. (The psalm might possibly connect to an occasion like that described in Nehemiah 12:27–43.) What in Psalm 147 might support this possibility?

2. What do you notice about this psalm that seems to ask us to divide it into three sections? How would you divide it, and what title and brief description would you give each section?

3. Besides the beginning of each section, what kinds of patterns do you notice in this poem? Examine its opening and closing and the ways in which its themes are organized as the poem develops.

4. What is the relentless focus of this psalm? How are most of the sentence structures similar—and what is the effect?

5. What is this psalm mainly about? How would you state the main idea of Psalm 147?

DAY THREE—FILLING IN THE PICTURE

1. Consider the claims of Psalm 147:1 concerning songs of praise to our God. In what ways does this psalm and the whole book of Psalms show these claims to be true?

2. Read Psalm 147:2–3, along with Isaiah 61:1–4 and Luke 4:16–21. How do these words reverberate with layers of meaning, starting with God's people back in Old Testament times, moving to God's people in New Testament times—and even extending to our own times?

3. Psalm 147:4–6 broadens dramatically, in a way common to patterns of biblical thinking. (In relation to these verses, consider Isaiah 40:26–28.) How might you explain the relationship of the different parts of Psalm 147:2–6?

4. Consider Psalm 147:7–11, which has a similar but reversed pattern.

   a. What do the pictures of Psalm 147:8–9 make you see—and make you understand about God?

   b. In Psalm 147:10–11, note the repeated word. What various things do we learn about God in these verses?

c. How might you sum up the main truth this whole two-part section teaches us about God?

5. The final section begins again with a focus on God's people—and ends with that focus as well.

a. Consider the picture of Jerusalem in Psalm 147:12–14, again asking how these words might reverberate with layers of meaning, starting back with God's people in Old Testament times and stretching ahead, through Christ—even to us today, as his church.

b. What is at the heart of this blessing of God's people? Psalm 147:15–20 has two different subsections, but they are held together by the idea of God's word. Examine and comment on how God's word moves through these verses like a strong, beautiful thread.

c. Stop to praise. Stop to consider the blessing of God's word, which called forth all creation, which upholds all creation, which established all his covenant promises in the Old Testament, and which brought the fulfillment of all those promises right down to us in the Word made flesh. Look back through this psalm, and write your personal response.

DAY FOUR—DIG IN YOURSELF (PSALM 148)

Psalm 148 again reaches out to the corners of creation—and again brings its praise right home to us. Consider the following questions and notes.

1. Upon prayerful reading and rereading, what initial <u>observations</u> would you make?

2. Consider the <u>context</u> of Psalm 148. *Note: Again the context is only that of God's people—which is really the point!*

3. What <u>shape</u> does this psalm have? *Note the beginning and ending, the discernible sections, and patterns and repetitions of words and ideas. There is at least one repeated word you cannot miss! In*

this psalm, note particularly the progression of participants in this praise. Why this order, from beginning to end?

4. Does a <u>main idea</u> begin to emerge? *Note: Keep coming back to this question as you make your way through the others.*

5. How do the <u>parallel lines</u> and the <u>imagery</u> communicate in this poem? *Note: In each psalm, different elements will stand out. Psalm 148:14, the final verse, stands out in its climactic beauty. Note that picture of the horn, which symbolizes strength. How is the concept of <u>nearness</u> especially vivid after the other verses of this psalm?*

6. In what ways does this psalm point us to <u>Christ</u>? *Possible passages to consider: Philippians 2:5–11; Luke 1:67–75; Revelation 5:8–14.*

7. What sorts of personal <u>applications and prayers</u> might you take away from this psalm?

(*Continued from previous page*)

(Continued from previous page)

Day Five—Take It In

Reread the two psalms you have studied in this lesson, and from them choose a verse or passage you would like to memorize. Write out the verse or passage and commit it to memory (or begin to do so!). Make these words a part of your thinking and your prayers. Be ready, if you wish, to share with your group why you chose these words and how they are working in your heart.

On this final day you might take a moment as well to review the verses you have chosen at the close of each lesson. Perhaps you will take with you from this study a desire to "hide in your heart" more passages from Psalms—maybe even whole psalms at a time. May this rich book of prayer and praise increasingly bless and nurture us, as we learn to join our voices with the universe-wide praise of our God, who showed his steadfast love to us in Jesus Christ, our Savior and our eternal King.

Notes for Leaders

What a privilege it is to lead a group in studying the Word of God! Following are six principles offered to help guide you as you lead.

1. The Primacy of the Biblical Text

If you forget all the other principles, I encourage you to hold on to this one! The Bible is God speaking to us, through his inspired Word—living and active and sharper than a two-edged sword. As leaders, we aim to point people as effectively as possible into this Word. We can trust the Bible to do all that God intends in the lives of those studying with us.

This means that the job of a leader is to direct the conversation of a group constantly back into the text. If you "get stuck," usually the best thing to say is: "Let's go back to the text and read it again...." The questions in this study aim to lead people into the text, rather than into a swirl of personal opinions about the topics of the text; therefore, depending on the questions should help. Personal opinions and experiences will often enrich your group's interactions; however, many Bible studies these days have moved almost exclusively into the realm of "What does this mean to me?" rather than first trying to get straight on "What does this mean?"

We'll never understand the text perfectly, but we can stand on one of the great principles of the Reformation: the *perspicuity* of Scripture. This simply means *understandability*. God made us word-creatures, in his image, and he gave us a Word that he wants us to understand more and more, with careful reading and study, and shared counsel and prayer.

The primacy of the text implies less of a dependence on commentaries and answer guides than often has been the case. I do not offer answers to the questions, because the answers are in the biblical text, and we desperately need to learn how to dig in and find them. When individuals articulate what they find for themselves (leaders included!), they have learned more, with each of their answers, about studying God's Word. These competencies are then transferable and applicable in every other study of the Bible. Without a set of answers, a leader will not be an "answer person," but rather a fellow searcher of the Scriptures.

Helps *are* helpful in the right place! It is good to keep at hand a Bible dictionary of some kind. The lessons themselves actually offer context and help with the questions as they are asked. A few commentaries are listed in the "Notes on Translations and Study Helps," and these can give further guidance after one has spent good time with the text itself. I place great importance as well on the help of leaders and teachers in one's church, which leads us into the second principle.

2. The Context of the Church

As Christians, we have a new identity: we are part of the body of Christ. According to the New Testament, that body is clearly meant to live and work in local bodies, local churches. The ideal context for Bible study is within a church body—one that is reaching out in all directions to the people around it. (Bible studies can be the best places for evangelism!) I realize that these studies will be used in all kinds of ways and places; but whatever the context, I would hope that the group leaders have a layer of solid church leaders around them, people to whom they can go with questions and concerns as they study the Scriptures. When a leader doesn't know the answer to a question that arises, it's really OK to say, "I don't know. But I'll be happy to try to find out." Then that leader can go to pastors and teachers, as well as to commentaries, to learn more.

The church context has many ramifications for Bible study. For example, when a visitor attends a study and comes to know the Lord, the visitor—and his or her family—can be plugged into the context of the church. For another example, what happens in a Bible study often can be integrated with other courses of study within the church, and even with the preaching, so that the whole body learns and grows together. This depends, of course, on the connection of those leading the study with those leading the church—a connection that I have found to be most fruitful and encouraging.

3. The Importance of Planning and Thinking Ahead

How many of us have experienced the rush to get to Bible study on time . . . or have jumped in without thinking through what will happen during the precious minutes of group interaction . . . or have felt out of control as we've made our way through a quarter of the questions and used up three-quarters of the time!

It is crucial, after having worked through the lesson yourself, to think it through from the perspective of leading the discussion. How will you open the session, giving perhaps a nutshell statement of the main theme and the central goals for the day? (Each lesson offers a brief introduction that will help with the opening.) Which questions do you not want to miss discussing, and which ones could you quickly summarize or even skip? How much time would you like to allot for the different sections of the study?

If you're leading a group by yourself, you will need to prepare extra carefully—and that can be done! If you're part of a larger study, perhaps with multiple small groups, it's helpful for the various group leaders to meet together and to help each other with the planning. Often, a group of leaders meets early on the morning of a study, in order to help the others with the fruit of their study, plan the group time, and pray—which leads into the fourth principle.

4. The Crucial Role of Prayer

If these words we're studying are truly the inspired Word of God, then how much we need to ask for his Spirit's help and guidance as we study his revelation! This is a prayer found often in Scripture itself, and a prayer God evidently loves to answer: that he would give us understanding of his truth, according to his Word. I encourage you as a leader to pray before and as you work through the lesson, to encourage those in your group to do the same, to model this kind of prayer as you lead the group time, to pray for your group members by name throughout the week, and to ask one or two "prayer warriors" in your life to pray for you as you lead.

5. The Sensitive Art of Leading

Whole manuals, of course, have been written on this subject! Actually, the four principles preceding this one may be most fundamental in cultivating your group leadership ability. Again, I encourage you to consider yourself not as a person with all the right answers, but rather as one who studies along with the people in your group—and who then facilitates the group members' discussion of all they have discovered in the Scriptures.

There is always a tension between pouring out the wisdom of all your own preparation and knowledge, on the one hand,

and encouraging those in your group to relish and share all they have learned, on the other. I advise leaders to lean more heavily toward the latter, reserving the former to steer gently and wisely through a well-planned group discussion. What we're trying to accomplish is not to cement our own roles as leaders, but to participate in God's work of raising up mature Christians who know how to study and understand the Word—and who will themselves become equipped to lead.

With specific issues in group leading—such as encouraging everybody to talk, or handling one who talks too much—I encourage you to seek the counsel of one with experience in leading groups. There is no better help than the mentoring and prayerful support of a wise person who has been there! That's even better than the best "how-to" manual. If you have a number of group leaders, perhaps you will invite an experienced group leader to come and conduct a practical session on how to lead.

Remember: the default move is, "Back to the text!"

6. THE POWER OF THE SCRIPTURES TO DELIGHT

Finally, in the midst of it all, let us not forget to delight together in the Scriptures! We should be serious but not joyless! In fact, we as leaders should model for our groups a growing and satisfying delight in the Word of God—as we notice its beauty, stop to linger over a lovely word or phrase, enjoy the poetry, appreciate the shape of a passage from beginning to end, laugh at a touch of irony or an image that hits home, wonder over a truth that pierces the soul.

May we share and spread the response of Jeremiah, who said:

> Your words were found, and I ate them,
>> and your words became to me a joy
>> and the delight of my heart. (Jer. 15:16)

Notes on Translations and Study Helps

This study can be done with any reliable translation of the Bible, although I do recommend the English Standard Version for its essentially literal but beautifully readable translation of the original languages. In preparing this study, I have used and quoted from the English Standard Version, published by Crossway Bibles in Wheaton, Illinois. Whichever additional translation you might choose, it will be most helpful if it consistently reflects the parallel structure of the original Hebrew poetry (see Lesson One).

These lessons may be completed with only the Bible open in front of you. The point is to grapple with the text, not with what others have said about the text. The goal is to know, increasingly, the joy and reward of digging into the Scriptures, God's breathed-out words, which not only are able to make us wise for salvation through faith in Christ Jesus, but also are profitable for teaching, reproof, correction, and training in righteousness, that each of us may be competent, equipped for every good work (2 Tim. 3:15–17).

To help you dig in, basic and helpful contexts and comments are given throughout the lessons. I have used and learned from the following books in my own study and preparation; you may find sources such as these helpful at some point.

General Handbooks:

The Crossway Comprehensive Concordance of the Holy Bible: English Standard Version. Compiled by William D. Mounce. Wheaton: Crossway Books, 2002. (Other concordances are available, from various publishers and for other translations.)

The Illustrated Bible Dictionary. 4 vols. Wheaton: Tyndale House Publishers, 1980. (*The Zondervan Pictorial Encyclopedia of the Bible* is similarly helpful.)

Ryken, Leland, James Wilhoit, and Tremper Longman III, eds. *Dictionary of Biblical Imagery.* Downers Grove, IL: InterVarsity Press, 1998.

Ryken, Leland, Philip Ryken, and James Wilhoit. *Ryken's Bible Handbook.* Wheaton: Tyndale House Publishers, 2005.

Vine's Complete Expository Dictionary of Old and New Testament Words. Nashville: Thomas Nelson, 1984.

Commentaries and Helps:

Boice, James Montgomery. *Psalms.* 3 vols. Grand Rapids: Baker Books, 1994.

Calvin, John. *Commentary on the Psalms.* Calvin's commentaries can be found in many different editions and also freely on the web. I access them through www.biblos.com (which offers many other helpful biblical tools and commentaries). They are made available to biblos.com through *Christian Classic Ethereal Library (www.ccel.org).*

Kidner, Derek. *Psalms.* Tyndale Old Testament Commentary. 2 vols. London: Inter-Varsity Press, 1973–1975.

Knight, George A. F. *Psalms.* Daily Bible Study Series Commentary. 2 vols. Philadelphia: Westminster, 1982–1983.

Spurgeon, Charles. *Treasury of David.* This commentary on the Psalms, like all Spurgeon's works, can be found in many different editions and also freely on the web. I access them through www.biblos.com. They are made available to biblos.com through *Internet Sacred Texts Archive (www.sacred-texts.com).*

Study Bibles:

ESV Study Bible. English Standard Version. Wheaton: Crossway Bibles, 2008.

The Literary Study Bible, English Standard Version. Wheaton: Crossway Bibles, 2007.

Kathleen Nielson (MA, PhD in literature, Vanderbilt University) has taught in the English departments at Vanderbilt University, Bethel College (Minnesota), and Wheaton College. She is the author of numerous Bible studies, the book *Bible Study: Following the Ways of the Word*, and various articles and poems. Kathleen has directed and taught women's Bible studies at several churches and speaks extensively at conferences and retreats. She serves as advisor and editor for The Gospel Coalition and was its director of women's initiatives from 2010–2017. She is also on the board of directors of The Charles Simeon Trust.

Kathleen and her husband Niel have three sons, two beautiful daughters-in-law, and a growing number of grandchildren!

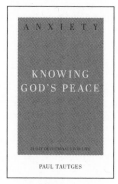

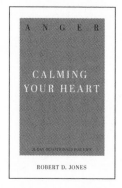
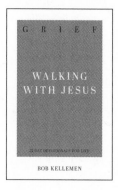

In the 31-Day Devotionals for Life series, biblical counselors and Bible teachers guide you through Scripture passages that speak to specific situations or struggles, helping you to apply God's Word to your life in practical ways day after day.

Devotionals endorsed by Brad Bigney, Kevin Carson, Mark Dever, John Freeman, Gloria Furman, Melissa Kruger, Mark Shaw, Winston Smith, Joni Eareckson Tada, Ed Welch, and more!

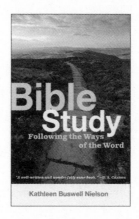

"Dissatisfied with leaving Bible study to the professionals while the rest of us are mere recipients of their work, Kathleen Nielson wants all Christians to be involved in thoughtful and faithful Bible study—and tells us how to do it."

—D. A. CARSON, Research Professor of New Testament, Trinity Evangelical Divinity School

"Nielson gives her readers a fresh and innovative, yet solid and God-glorifying approach to unlocking the truths of Scripture ... by reading God's words in order to ask what God is saying and how one should respond to him."

—DOROTHY PATTERSON, General Editor, *The Woman's Study Bible*

"The book cannot be better than it is ... it covers all the right topics in exactly the right order! For people who teach the Bible— or who aspire to teach it—this book will be the gold standard for knowing how to do it right."

—LELAND RYKEN, Professor of English, Wheaton College

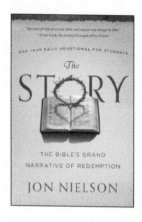

This yearlong study of God's Word guides you through five acts of his grand story of redemption. Although you won't read *every* chapter in the Bible, daily Scripture and devotional readings will equip you to understand the unity and development of God's story and to grow in your personal discipline of Bible study and prayer.

"*The Story* provides concise, clear, brief readings that will help anyone and everyone deepen their understanding of the big story of the Bible."

–Nancy Guthrie, Author, *The One Year Book of Discovering Jesus in the Old Testament*

"An incredible resource for students to thoughtfully read the Bible. It's true to Scripture, engaging, and concise yet thorough."

–Gloria Furman, Author, *Glimpses of Grace*